This book was transcribed from one of the thousands of sermons of Bill Vincent. Please realize this as you read this book. Thanks for your purchase and support.

The Goodness of God

Bill Vincent

Published by RWG Publishing, 2021.

While every precaution has been taken in the preparation of this book, the publisher assumes no responsibility for errors or omissions, or for damages resulting from the use of the information contained herein.

THE GOODNESS OF GOD

First edition. October 25, 2021.

Copyright © 2021 Bill Vincent.

Written by Bill Vincent.

Also by Bill Vincent

Building a Prototype Church: Divine Strategies Released
Experience God's Love: By Revival Waves of Glory School of the Supernatural
Glory: Expanding God's Presence
Glory: Increasing God's Presence
Glory: Kingdom Presence of God
Glory: Pursuing God's Presence
Glory: Revival Presence of God
Rapture Revelations: Jesus Is Coming
The Prototype Church: Heaven's Strategies for Today's Church
The Secret Place of God's Power
Transitioning Into a Prototype Church: New Church Arising
Spiritual Warfare Made Simple
Aligning With God's Promises
A Closer Relationship With God
Armed for Battle: Spiritual Warfare Battle Commands
Breakthrough of Spiritual Strongholds
Desperate for God's Presence: Understanding Supernatural Atmospheres
Destroying the Jezebel Spirit: How to Overcome the Spirit Before It Destroys You!
Discerning Your Call of God
Glory: Expanding God's Presence: Discover How to Manifest God's Glory

Glory: Kingdom Presence Of God: Secrets to Becoming Ambassadors of Christ
Satan's Open Doors: Access Denied
Spiritual Warfare: The Complete Collection
The War for Spiritual Battles: Identify Satan's Strategies
Understanding Heaven's Court System: Explosive Life Changing Secrets
A Godly Shaking: Don't Create Waves
Faith: A Connection of God's Power
Global Warning: Prophetic Details Revealed
Overcoming Obstacles
Spiritual Leadership: Kingdom Foundation Principles
Glory: Revival Presence of God: Discover How to Release Revival Glory
Increasing Your Prophetic Gift: Developing a Pure Prophetic Flow
Millions of Churches: Why Is the World Going to Hell?
The Supernatural Realm: Discover Heaven's Secrets
The Unsearchable Riches of Christ: Chosen to be Sons of God
Deep Hunger: God Will Change Your Appetite Toward Him
Defeating the Demonic Realm
Glory: Increasing God's Presence: Discover New Waves of God's Glory
Growing In the Prophetic: Developing a Prophetic Voice
Healing After Divorce: Grace, Mercy and Remarriage
Love is Waiting
Awakening of Miracles: Personal Testimonies of God's Healing Power
Deception and Consequences Revealed: You Shall Know the Truth and the Truth Shall Set You Free
Overcoming the Power of Lust
Are You a Follower of Christ: Discover True Salvation
Cover Up and Save Yourself: Revealing Sexy is Not Sexy
Heaven's Court System: Bringing Justice for All
The Angry Fighter's Story: Harness the Fire Within
The Wrestler: The Pursuit of a Dream

Beginning the Courts of Heaven: Understanding the Basics
Breaking Curses: Legal Rights in the Courts of Heaven
Writing and Publishing a Book: Secrets of a Christian Author
How to Write a Book: Step by Step Guide
The Anointing: Fresh Oil of God's Presence
Spiritual Leadership: Kingdom Foundation Principles Second Edition
The Courts of Heaven: How to Present Your Case
The Jezebel Spirit: Tactics of Jezebel's Control
Heaven's Angels: The Nature and Ranking of Angels
Don't Know What to Do?: Discover Promotion in the Wilderness
Word of the Lord: Prophetic Word for 2020
The Coronavirus Prophecy
Increase Your Anointing: Discover the Supernatural
Apostolic Breakthrough: Birthing God's Purposes
The Healing Power of God: Releasing the Power of the Holy Spirit
The Secret Place of God's Power: Revelations of God's Word
The Rapture: Details of the Second Coming of Christ
Increase of Revelation and Restoration: Reveal, Recover & Restore
Leadership vs Management
Restoration of the Soul: The Presence of God Changes Everything
Building a Prototype Church: The Church is in a Season of Profound of Change
Keys to Receiving Your Miracle: Miracles Happen Today
The Resurrection Power of God: Great Exploits of God
Transitioning to the Prototype Church: The Church is in a Season of Profound of Transition
Waves of Revival: Expect the Unexpected
The Stronghold of Jezebel: A True Story of a Man's Journey
Glory: Pursuing God's Presence: Revealing Secrets
Like a Mighty Rushing Wind
Steps to Revival
Supernatural Power
The Goodness of God

Watch for more at https://revivalwavesofgloryministries.com/.

The Goodness of God

God, I want you to fill my mouthful in Jesus' name, I don't want to just preach a word. I don't want to just dig up something and just preach it in Jesus' name. And Lord, I just want to give what you got and what you got is good Speaking of goodness, that's what we're going to talk about tonight. Because you are good, and how many know God is good. And God told me tonight, he said, as I was preparing a little bit, actually, I just got to prepare this morning. I went through kind of a little bit of non-sickness time. And that is a bit of confession anyway. So, this morning, I kind of woke up and I said, well, God it is the day I kind of need to need to tell me something like now All of a sudden, it just Whoosh. He said, talk about my goodness. And I said, God, you know, this is one of those times that you know, I'm just giving you a conversation because sometimes we need to hear the conversation. And I say, God, I said, well, you know, to talk about your goodness, right now you're good. I know you are. And I say that my face. But I said, there's been some blockage, there's been some hindrance, there's been a lot of things we've had to go around and go through lately. And I say, God, you know, this is not something that I'm physically feeling like I should be talking about right now. And he said, Listen, you're my prophet. And as you say it, I'll be, I'll begin to manifest my goodness. He said, remember when the revival began, and man, I love when we get into a conversation. How many loves to be in a conversation with Jehovah, God, King of glory. And we got in a conversation, and he came back. He said, remember at the beginning of the revival, you kept talking about the breakthrough. You preached about signs and wonders six months before signs and wonders manifested. you'd preached about this happening, this coming, and this happening, and it was before it manifested, he said, when you say it, it begins to manifest. So, he said, what I'm gonna do tonight is you're going to talk about my goodness, and his goodness is in the glory realm. How many want the glory hallelujah? The glory realm manifests His goodness. So, understand tonight, we're gonna just let God have his way. So, get ready to the taste of the Lord. See, he's good. Just imagine we're in a big giant theater and that's why we got a little echo. You were in a giant place. It's just taste of the Lord has seen he is good. And I'm telling you right now God is wanting us to taste of him. He can't be anything else but good. How many know he's well, even when he corrects? Ha-ha, He's good. His goodness is directly connected to His mercy and love. Once we have the revelation of His mercy and love will begin to have a big picture of who God is. And I'm telling you God is good. God's goodness knows no limits. God's goodness knows no limits. how many, how many have ever experienced God's goodness when you weren't supposed to? What I mean by that in the natural, you looked at yourself and you're saying I shouldn't be getting this. Sometimes God blesses you even when you don't deserve it. And I'm telling you, if there is one thing I know about my father in heaven, it's that he gives good gifts to his children. Not only good gifts but abundantly above what I can ask her to thank how many want the above the abundantly above. it's time for us to have a cup runneth over. it's time to have the land of milk and honey, it's time to have them over and above. That's what the Bible declares. Those who know their God will carry out great exploits. And knowing God is knowing his goodness knowing his love knowing everything good about him. The kind of God we serve does great exploits. He releases not only what we will have a need, but he also gets always gives us the 12 baskets leftover. are the seven baskets leftover, how long wherever he gives over and above? So, understand me. We got to have them over and above. I'm not going to be satisfied with just the need. I'm not going to be satisfied just to get the bills caught up. I'm not gonna be satisfied just to get the room covered tonight.

I'm not going to be satisfied with just the littles. I want the big one. We got the good God. So, let's go ahead and declare his good, hallelujah, and his mercies endure forever. And he's gonna begin to supply supernaturally for us. In God, it's always abundance. It's always supposed to be abundance in God. How many checkbooks look like abundance right now? I don't know about you, but those bills, look abundance to me. in the natural. those bills are nasty. They are the most faithful people in the world right now. they send one and then if you don't pay it, they send you another one to let you know that you didn't pay it. God is one to give us abundance. So let that truly resonate. resonate within you. I believe that God is going to set some of you free tonight. I receive it and bring you into the father's love. You're going to experience freedom from rejection and an all too familiar feeling of being distant from God. So, we got to understand a lot of us we are almost like living a spirit of rejection of God. When you're not living in his goodness, it's like you're feeling like he's leaving you. Like he's abandoned you. That's not our God. He doesn't do that. He doesn't give you a stone. He doesn't give you something that is dead works. He gives you good gifts. He will not withhold from his children. We are his children. If a teen girl back, there doesn't clean her room. That doesn't mean that she's not hurt child gone. That doesn't mean it's not. She's not still the mother's daughter. Just like we if we don't keep things just absolutely perfect. Does it mean we're still not as children? And what I mean by that is God is going to bring us to a place where we're going to be broken, have a spirit of rejection of him and begin to experience the one that he is, and he is good. Praise God. We give you praise. We thank You, Lord, for the increase. Surely goodness and mercy shall follow me all the days of my life. And I will dwell in the house of the Lord forever. You see, we're talking about God's mercy and loving-kindness all the days of our lives. It's not supposed to be just when the favors flow. When the increases there. It's supposed to be all the days of our lives are supposed to be in the times of new beginnings. They're supposed to be in the times of overflowing. It's supposed to be in times of desperation. It doesn't matter what road you're on, even if you're on the side road trying to get to the highway, wherever you are, we are supposed to be living in abundance. like someone said, and I agree with this. We are supposed to look like the king's kids. And I'm telling you it's time for us to experience the king's kid's benefits. Our benefits as children of the highest God are not based on the natural world. It doesn't matter how many times our president gets on the television and tells us how things are going to change. It doesn't matter how many times the unemployment rate goes up. It doesn't matter how much this happens in that happens. Doesn't matter. Anything else. What matters is we are that we are supposed to be based on that kingdom, not this kingdom. So, if we are based on the kingdom of heaven, we are to be provided supernaturally from God.

You see, you got to understand one of the things we put in here, I don't know if I can find it quickly. This was a picture of one of the signs and wonders that came in the ministry. A picture of a $100 bill that was in a woman's purse is an exact picture of that $100 bill. Now I understand. God could drop these by the abundance. Anytime. We could go out to our car, and instead of fast-food bags being on the floorboard, and be I don't know why I saw that but anyway, but it could be full of money. Could you imagine? Trying to get in the car and you got to scoot it over. You have to shut the door quickly to keep it in I don't know about you, but you say well, I don't know. Well, how many people during the revival had signs and wonders in their vehicles when they left that was locked. Lots of people had signs and wonders manifest on their car, in their dash in their floorboards that were locked in with the keys rentals up and I'm telling you over and over again God did these manifestations so and one of the women that testified of having one of those $100 bills was in her Bible at home. That's not something you bookmark your Bible with. And she did this, okay, I'm gonna say

THE GOODNESS OF GOD 5

just what happened. My stuff might fall out. But she, she took the Bible, she found it. She shook it because I saw it by the Spirit. And somebody called her to let her know she had a $100 bill in her Bible. She went, she found her Bible, she found it all to both ways. She shook it, she found it some more shook it some more. She goes, it's not in there. And I just manifested like I am always used to all the time. And I said it's in there I see it. She found it again. She shook it, she found it. And there was it's almost like God was already on his way. As I was seeing it. And there's not somebody that was flaky. It was somebody that was part of the team that got the $100 bill. And I'm telling you, God did these things over and over and over again. And I'm telling you, God can do anything however he wants to. But for some reason, in this season right now, it seems like that he's trying to get us to live about what is that word, live by. Yeah, it's that faith word. Is that being that? Is that one of those words? It should be a four-letter word, faith. But yeah, see? Yeah, it is an F word. All right. But I'm telling you, and we got to live by faith, and he is causing us to live by faith, but understand whether he does it in an abundance of $100 bills at your feet, whether he does it, put it in your Bible, put it in your purse, brings gemstones, signs, and wonders that you can cash in, I'm saying, let's say this, he can do whatever he wants to see, at this time, we still have gemstones, we have some gemstones that most of us have been manifested just in the home. But I understand they are good gifts to us.

You know, we probably hit a little something, something for him. But understand they're good gifts. So, it's not something that we just want to cash in. Halloween. It's not big, and it is. But God can bring anything to provide for us as children. But right now, he is doing it through a lot of other supernatural things. in, I'm telling you, he's gonna cause people to give under your hand, he's going to cause people to put things into your bank accounts, he's going to cause people to send money to go to your mailbox. He's going to cause insurance companies, power companies, electric companies, all the free money that they say is out there not going to have you look for it, but you're going to find out they look for you. And you're going to see interest in things that you were supposed to receive, you're going to find benefits of things that were forgotten about. but why? Because God's gonna cause favor of his goodness to come upon your life.

He is so willing and so eager. He's yearning to be good. Did you hear what I just said, God is yearning to be good to you. And to release his kindness and every need in your life, especially the area of healing. The wilderness of Jesus, think about that. Because you know that just as he said, I am willing to the leper, He is willing to you. does he need to say again and again and again, I'm willing? He is willing. He's moved with compassion. He doesn't want us to suffer. He doesn't want you to lack He wants you to have full provision. Many people struggle, struggle with the idea of having enough faith, trying to find more principles of healing. And just simply, you know, all we have to do is just simply accept the attitude that says I want to be healed and he's good. I'm healed You know, there are so many people out there that get conferences on how to get healed. we just got to get confident that he does it and we receive it. There's not a whole lot of real information in there. I mean, no matter how many ways you go around it, there are ways that you can be healed. There are ways that you need to forgive there are ways and all this different stuff. I agree with a lot of it. But I at the same time, you know, we can have a conference that says, we're going to give the secret to how to get healed. And then I could just preach that one line with that message. All right, I will preach one sermon, this is it, this is all you get. And this is going to be the final revelation that you're going to receive today. Just say, I'd like to be healed. Receive it is done. Thanks for coming. Pick up your tapes on the way out. I'm just joking. But I'm just saying we as a body of Christ, are trying to get more strategies and more emphasis on things that we don't need to get more emphasis on. And there's right now, I mean, there are so many in-time conferences that are contradicting one another. this guy says, we're going to leave in a twinkle of an eye before all the bad news. And there's another one that just says where our clothes are gonna drop, and we're gonna go, you know, it looks good on Hollywood, but it doesn't look good in the reality of the Bible.

And I'm telling you, and others say, we're going to live, leave, in the mid-trip, some are going to say, we're not, we're not going to leave till we all die. that's a good preacher. But I'm telling you, there's a lot of things out there. And most of it is just to dry fear in the body of Christ. I was traveling through looking because I don't have a television. So, I have internet, I was traveling through looking for some things by just by the Spirit, sometimes God tells me to look for, and I was looking for something on n times. And he told me that I'm going to show you something. And he said I got on to this one site. And I said in times, sermons, this coming service, and it opened up, they had a 15-minute commercial on buying barrels of food. barrels of water, filters for filtering your water out of a puddle, you can filter it to be 99%, your filter, and even your toilet water. And then they preached for 15 minutes. And then they had another 15-minute commercial at the end of it. So, it's a half-hour of commercials and a half and 15 minutes of teaching. And all it was, and God said all it is to make money. And it's working. It's big money. And the thing is, there's nothing wrong with getting a little bit of extra canned food in your house. There's nothing wrong with having an extra supply of water or this. But at the same time realize expiration. Bottled water is not good after a couple of years anyway. Trust me, we used to buy so much. And be like, well that's nasty. What happened to that? And it just, we got to understand sometimes we can live so much in fear, we waste what we have.

I remember we had an at the Ministry I was a part of. We had a like army surplus boxes food. One day I was in the mood for eggs, and I didn't have any eggs. So, I went out there and busted one of those boxes of liquid eggs and what they called them They weren't bad, he put about four pounds of salt on top of that, some ketchup. But anyway. But I'm just saying we got sometimes we got to use what we got. But at the same time, it's not supposed to bring us fear. And what God was showing me is there so many people aren't realizing the bigness of God. What I believe, is God is wanting to raise a generation, like no other generation who know their God and know that he's able to do great exploits. And we're going to get back to the days just like Moses, we can have manna from heaven, supernatural provision. If we need water, he's going to bring us water. He's going to bring a supernatural provision. At the same time there's nothing wrong with using wisdom there's nothing wrong with having a little bit of this or that happen Praise God. But at the same time and there is going to come a day I won't be banking, why? Because there's gonna come a day man one day and you won't be able to get any of your money. one day, it's done. And I'm telling you without the mark of the beast, there's going to be things like that's gonna happen, but at the same time, I'm not going to live in a spirit of fear. Because I got a big dog, and that's one of the things I want to put out there over the next season is, is we have a God who did great things in the word of God, but we read it like fairy tales. It's like just another story. It's not bedtime stories. Once upon a time, there was a guy named Moses and he had a big church. And they were messed up. So, God brought food from heaven. in that the way we read it, and they thought the way they preach it, it's like a fairy tale. And sounds pretty bad. But I'm telling you, I didn't. I didn't say it much different than a lot of preachers saying, because it's what happened. Now, what can happen? And signs and wonders and manifestations of unusual manifestations like God's doing are just a tickle just to let us know he can do anything.

 I have said I knew a guy who had his Bible. And he would, he'd set it on the seat and worship the Lord. And it got to the place, they would put a video camera to his seat. I saw this on his phone, he brought his phone and played a video and got to the place God manifested so often, always in the same scripture in revelations that talks about manna from heaven. And it's like popcorn, you just picked the Bible up inside from inside. And it was full of manner. And they would feed it to the entire congregation, there was always enough. Didn't matter if they had

7000, there would be 7000 pieces. there will always be more there will never be less. People went with seizures, different things. And I'm telling you, they eat it, and they were healed instantly. You say oh, we got to understand. I believe in a big God. And what I'm saying is His goodness comes upon the sons of God. Or the daughters of God. I'm just saying sons of God because it talks about being a heaven hit being sonship, I want to come into that sonship us men and women together can come into the sonship. If I can be the bride of Christ, you can be the sonship you can be the sons and I'll be the bride and we'll just get it all right, the guys are going to be the bride so we can all be sons, And I'm telling you, many people struggle with the idea of having enough faith, to try to find principles of healing. I'm telling you; I've already preached a little bit about this. But understand, I like to just be healed. be set free. And I know you are God. And I'm not. So, I'm not going to settle for this not being healed. Do you understand what I just said? So often we seem to have that mentality that I'll settle mentality. How many believe a lot of the body of Christ is settling. And I don't mean to sink because that's a whole nother sermon. settling. You know what I mean by structure kind of falls apart. cracks in drywall and some even feel guilty because their sickness isn't as bad as somebody else's.

I remember one time a woman didn't want to go up to the altar. Do you know why? Because the woman in the wheelchair didn't go up. She's like, I just got the sniffles. She's in a wheelchair. He's a big God. He can do both. as the woman in the wheelchair doesn't want to go up. I'm going up. If she wants to go up, I'm going up. I mean, I'm not gonna argue Come up with me or stand stay home, I don't care. I'm going up. And it's not putting it down. But we always get to the place. Well, so it's over there struggling with cancer. Lord, forgive me. No, we get all caught up in all these petty little things, and what I'm saying it's okay. For us to say this sometimes, but I'm telling you. The point that I'm trying to get to the point right now is so many of us say, God, it's okay. If you don't hear me, just heal them. We have a big God. What I'm saying is the body of Christ is constantly more or less asking God to limit himself. Just give what you got just give a little. You and I are children of God, sons, and daughters. We need to relate to God as his beloved. Um, his beloved. And I call it that way because it's a way of relating to that kind of relationship with God. sonship being his beloved is the sonship

Okay, Romans 8:15 I don't know if anybody wants to turn, I'm just kind of going through this tonight we're just going heavily I'll let you turn there if you want to. And I'm going to just talk briefly about my next point quick as you're turning their Romans 8:15 it's and the next point I'm going to talk about is the father's love sets us free it's the Father's love this set you free. Romans 8:15 says for you have not received the Spirit of bondage again to fear but you have received the Spirit of adoption where we cry, Aba, Father, how many you want to receive the Spirit of adoption we have as sons and daughters of the Most High God we have received adoption and I'm telling you are no longer the child of your natural mom and dad only everybody say hey man, talk about a curse that I got broke off of she's still my mom thank God But at the same time, I love that this we praise God I was in bed and rest in this way because of things I was feeling. And my mom came over and she had somebody come because she doesn't get around as good as she used to, she's using the slow lane And but anyway, she went out to praise God and she's happy always I mean I mean she's almost so happy to see me and praise God and we've been through a lot but man, everything's been just so good at the last, especially in this new beginning. And I'm telling you, but she goes you're not feeling well, and I say well I'm fighting something men. She goes, she goes, well you want me to pray for you, Bill. You know, it's kind of its kind of funny, you know because I'm like? I mean, but I go well, no, I'm okay. And she goes, she didn't even listen to me. She just says. Lord Jesus. Heal Bill right now. And Jesus mighty name. Amen. She goes, it was short, but it was from the heart. Oh, praise God. And I'm telling you, we got to understand God's goodness is good. And I thank God for our moms and dads. But He is my daddy. He's my Aba Father. He's my father in heaven. And I want to emphasize the word Aba father, because as the Father's love because we need to be able to relate to God is daddy. Some of the religious people, I started talking about him being daddy or Papa is man Oh, yeah, instantly. I mean, you got to understand daddy is good there's a song Rick Pino did. He did was goofing off in the revival. And he kind of just

we have the best dad in the whole world in the whole world. We have the best the dad. He just put it out there now really thinking anybody would pick it up. Everybody got excited about it. But I'm telling you, religious people, sometimes when they come to service, God tells me to pop it in because there we have the best dad in the whole world. And I'm telling you, and because we do. He is my best dad. With no disrespect to the dad, I had the most intimate term in the most intimate word you can find in the Bible, for God is Aba father. Which is daddy. If you want to think about it, it's daddy. I remember that. First. When I first got the revelation of this, I realized that I could come boldly before the throne of grace and say, Hey, Daddy, I'm home. Did you hear what I said? Man, it was exciting. I got confident I could come before boldly to the throne of grace. And I say, hey, Daddy, I'm home. What's up? Some of us need to get back to that relationship. Think about it. And I began to see what was kept. What was kept that what even kept the prodigal son and his older brother from receiving the goodness how treasures of the kingdom of heaven were the lack of revelation of the Father's love. We either have a revelation or the father's love. it tells us an illustration of His love and goodness when he sees your precedent for him and with all you might. He's going to show himself when you press, he shows I know when gold does manifest in a manifest most of the time still but when gold does manifest and a lot of people in the congregation, they would they say I go home, and I press them for 10 minutes and I look in the mirror and it's out there. It's like are your precedent for the gold dust or him? think about it You can understand Sometimes people got to tell me, I got it because I'm not going after that. It doesn't matter to me. Just makes me use more shampoo. It's because of his goodness, His goodness causes him to look for someone.

Anyone who loves him, so that he can bless them. Do you believe that the big Creator of the universe is over, going around looking, just looking? Who can I bless? who's the candidate to be blessed right now. is Tasha. Do you think Tasha is a candidate to be blessed? Tasha says I agree. I concur, Paula, do you think there is, any piece of your life right now that would say yes, I'm a candidate to be chosen to be blessed by God, the King of glory right now. No, that will, all the pieces. And I'm telling you, we got to understand that God wants to bless you. It's because of his goodness. that someone might be you. His eyes are running to and fro across the whole earth looking. Who can I bless? Who can I give? So right now, he's looking over the. This comes out of one of my books. But I like it. I like it by the Spirit. I put this in one of my books. But here's what he said. He said I'm looking over the balcony of heaven looking. Who can I bless? God's love. Just look off his balcony. On the big suite in heaven. And he's saying who can I bless today? I think I might be the Harris family. How about the Vincent family I don't know about here? But I want to put in a request. And he's looking over that balcony to come home. And I want to bless somebody is what he's saying. I want to give somebody mercy. And I want to be moved with compassion. I want to begin to release my love right now. And I want to release the father's love to the McDermott's. And I want to bless them and bless them and bless them. Jesus Christ, mercy, and compassion. We think about that to the widow we think about that to the orphan, we think about the invalid, the sick, the people who are going through the most difficult problems in our minds. But what about justice, children? God, I work for you. I work for you. I mean, everything I do I do unto you, even if you don't do everything that I do underhand the way I do it, that doesn't matter. You can work your business under him, you can do your job under him. you are a manager of what he gives you. and he blesses you for managing it. how many know the managers blessed when the house is blessed? Oh, let's go there a little bit. When you do business, and you do your management of what God gives you. According to him the way he wants you to. Even when you think you're just you're just being obedient with what he gives you.

He tells you to do something. I mean, in Centralia, he was like, give that away, give that away. give that away, give that away. I mean, I was given and given and given that night. I mean, man, I was like What in the world? go I said, I mean, first of all, we just traveled an hour and a half to get there. Last time, we barely had enough to get back and you're telling me just give, give and you know what they blew us away back It was good. It was good And I'm telling you, but God said Give this book away, give that book away give this city in this city in this city. And man, I just was like, Okay. Why? Because there's no comparison. I'm a manager of what he gives me. And what God's saying right now is, is when you manage and do well. What happens to a manager that does? Well, a lot of times he gets a promotion. Ooh, that's a good one promotion. he gets bonuses. Yeah, and he gets more he gets bonuses, he gets increased, he gets more increase. And I'm telling you whether or not it looks like you're doing well, with what you have. You've been a manager of what you have. Whether it's a little or a lot, you're a manager of it. So, you got to understand everything that I even think about. Even when I went to order this proof, I say, God, do I order the proof? You say Why? Because I'm a manager of my money. I don't just order proof just because I need one. I got books I need back there on the table. But I haven't got a release to order. It's been right. Because every time that I don't do something that normally my natural man would, that's when that money has been needed for something else. But I'm telling you, God is what brings us to a place right now to where I'm telling you there was about to be promoted, there's about to be the increase. There's about to be the bonuses, and there's about to be overflowing. Anything you can imagine or think. Because you're a child of a God who gives good gifts to his children. He's merciful. He is always moved with mercy and compassion to heal. The Bible says the sick people knew this. And some of them would come to Jesus asking for mercy. When you know he is going about doing things because of mercy, man, you get moved to go after it. To get some.

The Father loves you. The Father loves you. You got to hear this. The Father loves you. The same as he loved Jesus. say Jesus was the Son of God. So am I. I'm a son of God. I'm in the beloved. You got to understand. I'm not gonna call God my stepdad. I'm adopted, but I'm adopted. And he's dad. I'm adopted by the Spirit. And I'm telling you, and I call him dad. He is my ABA father. I may have not been produced through a virgin like Jesus was but I am still his son. And I have the same rights. And I'm telling you to praise God. Even these girls back here, I will never replace their daddy, their daddy. And that right? These girls back here, Haley and McCann I'm telling you their daddy is their daddy and they'll always have daddy as daddy, and I'll never replace him ever in a million years. But I love these girls as my own when I can't do things and supply and order things and do this and that. I'm like, I want to be able to bless them. I didn't even know I had the feeling I have, I'm like what world who knew a few years ago in the midst of revival I'd be doing soccer games and, and all these things that I do now the one on the soccer games and worrying about somebody who's at the emergency room with a broken, cracked hand. Things like this are a whole different arena for me. But understand the King of glory. God in heaven looks down upon you as his children just as much as Jesus is his child. Think about that son and daughter. Do you think there was ever a time when our heavenly father didn't listen to Jesus?

Did you hear what I just said? Think about that. And when you think about that, think about this is your heavenly Father going to turn a deaf ear to you. So, we need to behave like sons and daughters. We got to think about something. Some people see Jesus, his life is all Milk and Honey, you know what God just taught? Show me that this week. He said, I want you to look at this, I want you to look at that. And I want you to look at this. And I want you to look at that. And he said, See, he was my only begotten Son. Think about this. And he saw and knew by the Spirit, what was about to happen to him? When he said, if this cup may not pass from me, I will drink. He was taking and tempted. he was taking and experiencing the highest form of temptation that any man could face. And he was taken and not before he was ever beaten, he could see that it was coming. And he still chose to go ahead. Yes, there were days when they were waving olms that he was the king. There were days whenever people would surround him, and just love to hang on to every word that he had. There were days whenever people would flock just to go from city to city and follow him wherever he would go. But there were also days where everyone turned her back on him. There were days. And one day specifically when he cried out to God in heaven. Why have thou forsaken me? But he still wasn't the guy that stood, showed himself to the disciples, with the holes in his hands and feet.

So, some of us look at Jesus as this glorious man and never faced anything. I believe he sweat. I believe he cried. probably cried more than anybody. You got to realize this happened in three and a half years what we read. I wasn't that. I mean, he had a whole lot more work bad things that seem like they're good things. Not to mention, when he began to come forth, they said, Oh, you're just a carpenter. So, rejection before even getting started. So, God took me through this, looking at the other flip side of Jesus, and all the different things that happened. And you know what? He said, see and understand that it was like he went through glory. Valley, glory, valley, glory, valley. But he ended in the highest rung of glory. And he said to me this because this is what I'm finishing with. My highest men and women of God. generals of God, pioneers of God. They are tested and approved. They're the ones that make it through when it looks like they should quit. Because of that, the father loves you. Just as much as he loved him and still loves him. I want you to begin to ask, seek, knock. The Father in heaven loves you and He wants to do abundantly above anything. You can ask her to think he wants to satisfy your mouth with good things. he wants your mouth to be full of good stuff. How many know, it's not so easy to be full of good stuff sometimes. Receive your love. Receive your love, receive the mercy and goodness of God just allow the truth of the Father's love, and he loves you, just as he loved Jesus, He loves you. Let Jesus bring rest to your soul. Let the revelation of the, of how special you are to the Lord. You got to realize our brother, so to speak. Jesus was staying here for us. If it wasn't for Jesus, our salvation would not be even the way it is now. If it wasn't for Jesus, that prophetic, pure shore Word of the Lord would not be in place the way it is now. Jesus is a personality of God that we got to know and get to keep all the days of our life.

He's our brother, he's, our kin. I'm on there to teach you one time on generational blessings. We always hear about the generational curses. Well, I have a generational blessing. I got good kin. Jesus is my kin. So, I can receive the generational blessing? Sure. Yeah. Have you ever thought of the question? If I only had one more opportunity left? What would I say to the people I love? Everybody Think about that. If you only have one more opportunity to say something to the person you love, to people you love. What would it be? Would it be? Can I go to justice? I didn't know what justice was either. But I do know It's mainly a girl store. But that's beside the point. The reason I'm asking you this. I asked this because I believe if God only had one more opportunity to speak to you, he would tell you just how much you mean to him? Because he is good. And his love endures forever. He might look at you and say Yeah. And the natural he could say you've kind of wind a lot lately. You've kind of threatened me that you were going to quit again. And you might even through that said I quit threw in the towel just went ahead and quit again. But in the midst of all that he still will look you square in the eye and say, I love you. See, we got to understand most people don't understand the real compassion and love God has for us. And if you know His goodness, you know his love. Why? Because most of the churches are religious. It's gotten to a place it's all about showmanship works.

How well do I dress is the Usher elder Deacon? There is another very important thing. I remember when it comes to God's goodness is because of his goodness, that he always does his utmost to convict me. He is good because he convicts me, I didn't say I was all going to be bushy-tailed, we're gonna be ending with a good. That's a good thing. Because it's the children that do things and keep doing things that their parents don't care what they do. They don't feel the love. It's the children that are in the streets running up and down the streets and the parents never look out the window. that aren't getting the love, feeling the love for the father and the mother. We are children. And you can testify of this. When you're convicted. that should just testify, you ought to be like, Man, I'm good. I'm good with him. If he's convicted me, that means I'm here is it's when he's not convicted you that's when you need to worry. Somebody said to me one time I preached on temptation, they go, I'm never tempted. I go really. I said you don't ever have a conviction of the Holy Spirit or anything. And they said no. I said, are you saved? They said, no, I, I just look good. I was so consumed and unnatural. I didn't even want to tap into the spirit. I was like, man, I don't even want to talk to you no more, just go away

God always wants us to be in the right position to receive the Holy Spirit's work of conviction. It's because of his goodness that we receive the grace, to repent. And I'm telling you, he doesn't want to just Bless you. He wants to convict you too. Oh, doesn't that make you feel good? See, we got to understand I remember one time my brother, my natural dad passed away when I was six. And so, I lived in a lot of years without a daddy at all. But as a young man, I got to roam and wander as my mom couldn't keep up with me. And I was very young, but I was pretty innocent. I just like to get on the bike and go and go and go and go and go and sometimes be 10 miles away. But that's the way I was I was a roamer is what everybody called me. Well, one day, my brother happened to be around, and he caught me and got me back home and he whipped me. And he said I'm doing this because I love you. Now how many know at the time I didn't understand what I'm like? I mean, you're doing this now because I wasn't crying. He picked up a book and used it to I guess it had to hurt Since I wasn't responding to the slaps. He just went ahead and got the big book out off the table. That one hurt So, and once, I realized that was part of the deal, I was gonna have to jerk a tear to I was a kid, but he said that, and you know, I thought about that. And he said I want you to think about that and stay in this room until you know why I said that to you. And he came, I came out the door. He looked up and he's already in a good mood and getting dinner ready or whatever. And all of a sudden, he said, I did that. Why? I said I know you did it because you love me.

You don't want me to be like you. You don't want me to follow the world and just do whatever I want. He said, Good enough. You got to understand. Praise God This is one brother who had at this time had seven DUIs been arrested by a lot, you know, did a lot of things. And I was still a kid and he saw that the things that he started doing when he was a kid, I was doing so he whipped me to let me know. That wasn't right. You can't go in this direction. Sometimes children don't understand if we tell them things not to do. Because we know some things. How many know sometimes we know some things. We might not know everything, but we know some things like the law of gravity. We understand the law of gravity. What goes up comes do, how many know sometimes as children, we don't understand that. We're like I'm just going to jump this ramp and see how high I can go. We don't think about the landing. the reason I'm saying this tonight is that God is wanting to bring us to the His goodness, praise God, I have more, but I'm not preaching more I want to receive His goodness I want to receive his glorious goodness. And that comes with convictions. That comes with God looking at you by the Spirit of God, and saying, you shouldn't have done that. How many have ever more or less complained to God about something and then felt bad about it later? I mean, I don't know. I mean, any honest people? Sometimes it's like God doesn't even see me. I mean, I'm writing all these books, and you're just like, Praise God. The reason I'm saying some of these things is because God wants us to get to a place to experience His goodness again. I mean, fully all the time. He can blow you away. I don't know about you. But I want to step into your field of blowing my mind. But it comes with the convictions. It's not just in the glory, it's also the convictions. It's not just saying God is going to come down and supply all your needs through provision through checks in the mail, through all this type of thing. supernatural revision, somebody slipping hundreds in your hand. It's not like that, only. It's also him just bringing something for you to feel I got to get right. I got to repent. I shouldn't be that angry. I shouldn't be that upset. I shouldn't have said that. I shouldn't have done that.

    Praise God. Lord, we receive, we want to be full measure your child. And what that means is not just to receive from your hand. But it's also to receive your phrase. Yes, you are to be our provider to supply our needs. But also, to supply abundantly above all we can ask or think. And we received that. I received this as, as you said, a prophetic word tonight. I'm prophesied that your goodness shall follow us all the days of our life. But in your goodness, also his convictions. We need to spend more time we need to go to God about more of what we use the money for. We will tie and give offerings also. The biggest thing about being a good manager of money is tithes and offerings. There are so many people in the church at one time, I'm telling you, they used to get upset. I'm not talking about it in my churches, but in other people's churches where I was a minister within those churches. And I'm telling you that we get upset people that didn't give their tithes and offering would be the most lack people and be upset about it. You don't give tithes and offerings. Pretty much you're just saying no to the benefits. I don't know about you, but we got to have a lining up and they would even try to say within the word of God, this does not mean that we're supposed to give 10% and one day I preached I said, Yeah, actually, I believe it's more around 20%. But we're not gonna go there today. Or yet. And then I go, yes, we did, didn't we? Because see, it's not about just, and I have lived in times where I have ties. So big out of my own money. There were times I didn't have hardly any money. There was one time I was making like $135 a week, I'm telling you, I would give, I would give 17 to 18% at that time because I did have a full revelation of all that God wanted me to do. And I'm telling you I had more money than I ever had. I was like, why am I so blessed, and God says because you're lining up to my word, I'm not saying this to get your ties tonight this is not I'm not the local church But I'm telling you God is doing something. And what I am saying is I can do more with 90% than I can with 100% I can do more when I saw in good ground. God is good. God is good. Any good Praise God.

Don't miss out!

Visit the website below and you can sign up to receive emails whenever Bill Vincent publishes a new book. There's no charge and no obligation.

https://books2read.com/r/B-A-XHBC-GFXSB

BOOKS 2 READ

Connecting independent readers to independent writers.

Also by Bill Vincent

Building a Prototype Church: Divine Strategies Released
Experience God's Love: By Revival Waves of Glory School of the Supernatural
Glory: Expanding God's Presence
Glory: Increasing God's Presence
Glory: Kingdom Presence of God
Glory: Pursuing God's Presence
Glory: Revival Presence of God
Rapture Revelations: Jesus Is Coming
The Prototype Church: Heaven's Strategies for Today's Church
The Secret Place of God's Power
Transitioning Into a Prototype Church: New Church Arising
Spiritual Warfare Made Simple
Aligning With God's Promises
A Closer Relationship With God
Armed for Battle: Spiritual Warfare Battle Commands
Breakthrough of Spiritual Strongholds
Desperate for God's Presence: Understanding Supernatural Atmospheres
Destroying the Jezebel Spirit: How to Overcome the Spirit Before It Destroys You!
Discerning Your Call of God
Glory: Expanding God's Presence: Discover How to Manifest God's Glory

Glory: Kingdom Presence Of God: Secrets to Becoming Ambassadors of Christ
Satan's Open Doors: Access Denied
Spiritual Warfare: The Complete Collection
The War for Spiritual Battles: Identify Satan's Strategies
Understanding Heaven's Court System: Explosive Life Changing Secrets
A Godly Shaking: Don't Create Waves
Faith: A Connection of God's Power
Global Warning: Prophetic Details Revealed
Overcoming Obstacles
Spiritual Leadership: Kingdom Foundation Principles
Glory: Revival Presence of God: Discover How to Release Revival Glory
Increasing Your Prophetic Gift: Developing a Pure Prophetic Flow
Millions of Churches: Why Is the World Going to Hell?
The Supernatural Realm: Discover Heaven's Secrets
The Unsearchable Riches of Christ: Chosen to be Sons of God
Deep Hunger: God Will Change Your Appetite Toward Him
Defeating the Demonic Realm
Glory: Increasing God's Presence: Discover New Waves of God's Glory
Growing In the Prophetic: Developing a Prophetic Voice
Healing After Divorce: Grace, Mercy and Remarriage
Love is Waiting
Awakening of Miracles: Personal Testimonies of God's Healing Power
Deception and Consequences Revealed: You Shall Know the Truth and the Truth Shall Set You Free
Overcoming the Power of Lust
Are You a Follower of Christ: Discover True Salvation
Cover Up and Save Yourself: Revealing Sexy is Not Sexy
Heaven's Court System: Bringing Justice for All
The Angry Fighter's Story: Harness the Fire Within
The Wrestler: The Pursuit of a Dream

Beginning the Courts of Heaven: Understanding the Basics
Breaking Curses: Legal Rights in the Courts of Heaven
Writing and Publishing a Book: Secrets of a Christian Author
How to Write a Book: Step by Step Guide
The Anointing: Fresh Oil of God's Presence
Spiritual Leadership: Kingdom Foundation Principles Second Edition
The Courts of Heaven: How to Present Your Case
The Jezebel Spirit: Tactics of Jezebel's Control
Heaven's Angels: The Nature and Ranking of Angels
Don't Know What to Do?: Discover Promotion in the Wilderness
Word of the Lord: Prophetic Word for 2020
The Coronavirus Prophecy
Increase Your Anointing: Discover the Supernatural
Apostolic Breakthrough: Birthing God's Purposes
The Healing Power of God: Releasing the Power of the Holy Spirit
The Secret Place of God's Power: Revelations of God's Word
The Rapture: Details of the Second Coming of Christ
Increase of Revelation and Restoration: Reveal, Recover & Restore
Leadership vs Management
Restoration of the Soul: The Presence of God Changes Everything
Building a Prototype Church: The Church is in a Season of Profound of Change
Keys to Receiving Your Miracle: Miracles Happen Today
The Resurrection Power of God: Great Exploits of God
Transitioning to the Prototype Church: The Church is in a Season of Profound of Transition
Waves of Revival: Expect the Unexpected
The Stronghold of Jezebel: A True Story of a Man's Journey
Glory: Pursuing God's Presence: Revealing Secrets
Like a Mighty Rushing Wind
Steps to Revival
Supernatural Power
The Goodness of God

Watch for more at https://revivalwavesofgloryministries.com/.

About the Author

Bill Vincent is no stranger to understanding the power of God. Not only has he spent over twenty years as a Minister with a strong prophetic anointing, he is now also an Apostle and Author with Revival Waves of Glory Ministries in Litchfield, IL. Along with his wife, Tabitha, he, leads a team providing apostolic oversight in all aspects of ministry, including service, personal ministry and Godly character.

Bill offers a wide range of writings and teachings from deliverance, to experiencing presence of God and developing Apostolic cutting edge Church structure. Drawing on the power of the Holy Spirit through years of experience in Revival, Spiritual Sensitivity, and deliverance ministry, Bill now focuses mainly on pursuing the Presence of God and breaking the power of the devil off of people's lives.

His books 50 and counting has since helped many people to overcome the spirits and curses of Satan. For more information or to keep up with Bill's latest releases, please visit www.revivalwavesofgloryministries.com. To contact Bill, feel free to follow him on twitter @revivalwaves.

Read more at https://revivalwavesofgloryministries.com/.

About the Publisher

Accepting manuscripts in the most categories. We love to help people get their words available to the world.

Revival Waves of Glory focus is to provide more options to be published. We do traditional paperbacks, hardcovers, audio books and ebooks all over the world. A traditional royalty-based publisher that offers self-publishing options, Revival Waves provides a very author friendly and transparent publishing process, with President Bill Vincent involved in the full process of your book. Send us your manuscript and we will contact you as soon as possible.

Contact: Bill Vincent at rwgpublishing@yahoo.com www.rwgpublishing.com

www.ingramcontent.com/pod-product-compliance
Lightning Source LLC
LaVergne TN
LVHW042005060526
838200LV00041B/1880